RANJOT SINGH CHAHAL

Growth Mindset Mastery

Overcome, Connect, and Grow

Rana Books

First published by Rana Books (UK, India) 2023

First edition

ISBN: 978-81-19786-25-1

Contents

Chapter 1: The Power of Positivity

Section 1: Understanding Positive Thinking

Positive thinking is a psychological and emotional state characterized by an optimistic outlook on life. It involves focusing on favorable outcomes searching for silver linings and cultivating a mindset that sees possibilities and opportunities even in challenging situations. Positive thinking is not about denying or disregarding negative or difficult experiences; rather it is about embracing a constructive perspective that enables personal growth and resilience.

1.1 The Nature of Positive Thinking

Positive thinking encompasses various cognitive processes including self-talk cognitive reappraisal and reframing. Self-talk refers to the internal dialogue we have with ourselves where we can either reinforce negative beliefs or replace them with positive affirmations. Cognitive reappraisal involves reevaluating the meaning or interpretation of a situation allowing us to find positive aspects we might have initially overlooked. Reframing involves changing the way we perceive a problem or challenge viewing it as an opportunity for growth rather than a setback.

1.2 The Power of Positive Thoughts

Our thoughts have a profound impact on our emotions behaviors and overall well-being. Negative thoughts can fuel stress anxiety and pessimism hindering personal development and affecting our relationships. Conversely positive thoughts can enhance happiness resilience and general life satisfaction.

Research shows that positive thinking can improve physical health. For example a study conducted by the University of Wisconsin-Madison found that people who practiced positive thinking had a lower risk of developing cardiovascular disease. Positive thinkers tend to have healthier coping mechanisms such as exercising maintaining a balanced diet and seeking social support which contribute to overall well-being.

1.3 The Role of Perception in Positive Thinking

Perception plays a vital role in positive thinking. How we perceive and interpret events determines our emotional reactions and subsequent behaviors. By reframing our perception we can transform negative experiences into valuable lessons or opportunities for personal growth.

For instance imagine you fail to meet a deadline at work. A person with a negative perspective might see this as a sign of incompetence and a potential threat to their job security. In contrast a person with a positive perspective might view it as a chance to learn from their mistakes improve time management skills and seek guidance from colleagues to ensure future success.

1.4 Positive Thinking and Internal Locus of Control

Positive thinking often stems from having an internal locus of control which is the belief that we have control over our lives and can influence the outcomes we experience. Internal locus of control empowers individuals to take personal responsibility for their thoughts emotions and actions leading to a greater sense of agency and positivity.

For example imagine two individuals face a challenging situation at work. The one with an internal locus of control believes they have the ability to overcome obstacles learn from failures and succeed through their efforts. The other person with an external locus of control blames external factors for their difficulties and feels helpless. The person with an internal locus of control is more likely to adopt positive thinking strategies seeing the situation as an opportunity for growth while the person with an external locus of control may succumb to negativity and a sense of helplessness.

Section 2: Benefits of Maintaining a Positive Attitude

Maintaining a positive attitude has numerous benefits across various aspects of life. Here are some notable advantages:

2.1 Emotional Well-being

Positive thinking enhances emotional well-being by reducing stress anxiety and depression. When faced with difficult situations individuals with a positive attitude are more resilient and better equipped to cope with challenges. They can reframe negative experiences focusing on lessons learned or potential solutions rather than dwelling on the negativity.

2.2 Improved Relationships

Positive thinking promotes healthier and more fulfilling relationships. People naturally gravitate toward positive individuals as they exude optimism encouragement and support. Maintaining a positive attitude enables effective communication empathy and better problem-solving within personal and professional relationships.

For instance consider a situation in which two friends experience setbacks in their respective careers. A person with a positive attitude can provide support empathy and motivation to their friend reinforcing a sense of belief in their abilities and encouraging them to explore alternative opportunities. This positive energy strengthens the bond between friends and fosters a nurturing environment.

2.3 Enhanced Resilience

Positive thinking enhances resilience allowing individuals to bounce back from setbacks and adversity. When facing challenges those with a positive attitude view them as temporary hurdles rather than insurmountable obstacles. They maintain their composure adapt their strategies and seek opportunities for growth.

For example think of a professional athlete who sustains an injury. A positive-minded athlete may use the setback as an opportunity to focus on other aspects of their training or explore new techniques to enhance performance. This mindset allows them to maintain motivation and bounce back stronger and more resilient than before.

2.4 Increased Motivation and Productivity

Positive thinking generates a sense of motivation and productivity. When individuals believe in their abilities to succeed they approach tasks with enthusiasm and determination. They are more likely to set goals visualize success and persist in the face of challenges.

For instance consider two employees assigned a challenging project at work. The employee with a positive attitude will approach the task with enthusiasm seeing it as an opportunity to showcase their skills and contribute to the organization's success. This motivation drives them to work diligently seek innovative solutions and go the extra mile to achieve outstanding results.

2.5 Improved Physical Health

Positive thinking is not only beneficial for emotional well-being but it also positively impacts physical health. Research suggests that positive thinking is associated with lower levels of stress hormones improved immune system functioning and reduced risk of various health conditions.

For example a study conducted by the University of Kentucky found that individuals who had a positive outlook on life had a decreased risk of developing hypertension (high blood pressure). Positive thinkers often engage in healthier habits like exercise proper nutrition and adequate sleep contributing to better overall physical health.

In conclusion positive thinking is a powerful psychological and emotional tool that can enhance various aspects of life. By understanding positive thinking and its underlying mechanisms individuals can harness its benefits and improve their well-being. Cultivating a positive attitude allows us to perceive challenges as opportunities improve relationships enhance resilience increase motivation and productivity as well as improve physical health. Embracing positive thinking not only transforms our inner world but also influences how we perceive and navigate the external world leading to a more fulfilling and meaningful life.

Chapter 2: Overcoming Challenges

Section 1: Strategies for Resilience

Resilience is the ability to bounce back and thrive in the face of adversity. Life is full of challenges setbacks and unexpected events but it is our resilience that allows us to adapt learn and grow from these experiences. In this section we will explore some strategies for building resilience and overcoming challenges.

1. Cultivating a Growth Mindset:

Having a growth mindset is essential for resilience. It is the belief that our abilities and intelligence can be developed through effort learning and perseverance. People with a growth mindset see failures and setbacks as opportunities for growth and learning rather than indications of their intelligence or worth. They embrace challenges view feedback as constructive and are more likely to persevere when faced with obstacles. For example instead of saying "I am not good at this someone with a growth mindset would say "I can improve with practice and effort."

2. Building a Strong Support Network:

Having a strong support network is crucial during challenging times. Surrounding yourself with friends family mentors or support groups that offer encouragement advice and emotional support can make a significant difference in overcoming obstacles. Sharing challenges and seeking guidance from others can provide new perspectives insights and solutions. Moreover a support network provides a sense of belonging and helps reduce stress enhancing one's ability to cope with difficulties.

3. Developing Emotional Intelligence:

Emotional intelligence (EQ) is the ability to recognize understand and manage our own emotions as well as understand and empathize with the emotions of others. Building emotional intelligence can help us navigate challenges more effectively by understanding and regulating our emotions communicating effectively and building strong relationships. For example during a setback being aware of our emotions such as frustration or disappointment allows us to take proactive steps to manage those emotions constructively rather than letting them overwhelm us.

4. Practicing Self-Care:

Taking care of oneself is essential for resilience. Engaging in activities that promote physical mental and emotional well-being helps build the necessary energy and strength to navigate challenges. Self-care includes getting enough sleep eating a balanced diet maintaining an exercise routine and engaging in activities that bring joy and relaxation. Regular self-care practices support resilience by improving overall well-being and helping to manage stress effectively.

5. Developing Problem-Solving Skills:

Developing problem-solving skills is crucial in overcoming challenges. It involves identifying the issue analyzing possible solutions and taking action. Being proactive and finding solutions rather than dwelling on the problem helps build resilience and a sense of empowerment. Problem-solving skills can be cultivated through practice and by seeking guidance from others. For instance if facing a financial setback brainstorming possible strategies like seeking additional sources of income or reducing expenses can help overcome the challenge effectively.

6. Maintaining a Positive Outlook:

Maintaining a positive outlook does not mean ignoring or denying difficulties. Instead it involves reframing challenges as opportunities for growth and focusing on solutions rather than dwelling on the negative aspects. Optimism helps in building resilience by increasing motivation enhancing problem-solving abilities and fostering a sense of hope in challenging situations. For example instead of thinking "This setback will ruin everything a positive outlook would focus on the potential opportunities that may arise from the setback.

Section 2: Turning Setbacks into Opportunities

Setbacks are a natural part of life and often they provide valuable opportunities for growth and development. In this section we will explore how setbacks can be turned into opportunities.

1. Learning from Failure:

Failure is often seen as something to be avoided but it is an essential part of growth and success. Setbacks and failures provide valuable lessons and opportunities for learning. Reflecting on what went wrong identifying areas for improvement and adjusting our strategies can lead to personal growth and ultimately to success. Thomas Edison after numerous failures famously said "I have not failed. I've just found 10000 ways that won't work." Embracing failure as a learning experience fuels resilience and opens doors for new opportunities.

2. Embracing Change and Adaptation:

Setbacks often require us to adapt and make changes. Embracing change and being open to new possibilities helps us overcome challenges by finding alternative paths to success. Being flexible and adaptable allows us to navigate obstacles effectively and make the most of unexpected situations. For example a business that faces a decline in demand for a particular product may choose to pivot and explore new markets or develop new products turning the setback into an opportunity for innovation and growth.

3. Developing New Skills:

Setbacks can be an opportunity to develop new skills and broaden our abilities. When faced with challenges it is often necessary to acquire new knowledge or skills to overcome them. Taking advantage of setback situations to learn new skills enroll in training programs or seek guidance from experts can not only help us overcome the challenges at hand but also enhance our personal and professional growth in the long run.

4. Building Resilience and Perseverance:

Setbacks provide an opportunity to build resilience and perseverance. The ability to bounce back from failures and setbacks strengthens our character and fortitude. It helps us develop a "never give up" attitude and the determination to keep going despite obstacles. Setbacks can act as a test of our resilience and offer an opportunity to push beyond our comfort zones. Thomas Edison's quote perfectly encapsulates this idea "Genius is 1% inspiration and 99% perspiration."

5. Finding New Opportunities:

Sometimes setbacks can lead to unexpected opportunities. When one door closes another one often opens. It is essential to maintain a positive mindset and actively seek out potential opportunities that may arise from setbacks. For example being laid off from a job can be an opportunity to explore new career paths or start a business venture. By staying open-minded and adaptable setbacks can transform into stepping stones for personal and professional growth.

In conclusion overcoming challenges and turning setbacks into opportunities require resilience a positive mindset and proactive strategies. Developing a growth mindset building a support network cultivating emotional intelligence practicing self-care developing problem-solving skills and maintaining a positive outlook are key strategies for building resilience. Setbacks on the other hand can be turned into opportunities by learning from failures embracing change and adaptation developing new skills building resilience and perseverance and finding new opportunities. By adopting these strategies and embracing setbacks as opportunities we can grow learn and thrive in the face of challenges.

Chapter 3: Nurturing Relationships

Chapter 3: Nurturing Relationships

Section 1: Building Strong Connections

Building strong connections and nurturing relationships is an essential aspect of our personal and professional lives. Whether it's with our family friends colleagues or even strangers the quality of our relationships greatly influences our happiness well-being and success. In this section we will explore the various components that contribute to building strong connections and fostering meaningful relationships.

1. Trust and Authenticity: Trust is the foundation of any healthy relationship. When we trust someone we feel safe secure and comfortable expressing ourselves. It is crucial to be authentic and genuine in our interactions to build trust. This means being open and honest sharing our thoughts and feelings while also respecting the boundaries and privacy of others. For example being open about our vulnerabilities admitting our mistakes and showing empathy towards others can help establish trust and authenticity in our relationships.

2. Shared Values and Interests: People naturally gravitate towards those who share similar values and interests. Shared values provide a sense of alignment and understanding while shared interests offer opportunities for engaging experiences and activities. For instance if two individuals have a passion for music they can attend concerts together share favorite songs or even start a music club. Finding common ground and participating in shared activities facilitates deeper connections and creates stronger bonds.

3. Empathy and Understanding: Empathy is the ability to understand and share another person's feelings and experiences. It plays a significant role in building strong connections. When we empathize with others we demonstrate that we care and value their emotions. This can be achieved by actively listening putting ourselves in their shoes and responding with compassion and understanding. For example if a friend is going through a tough time we can offer support by lending a listening ear providing comfort and offering assistance if needed. Engaging in empathetic behaviors strengthens relationships and fosters a sense of belonging.

4. Mutual Respect and Support: Building strong connections requires mutual respect and support. Respecting others means recognizing their worth individuality and personal boundaries. It involves treating others with kindness courtesy and patience even when there are differences in opinions or beliefs. Additionally providing support and encouragement to our loved ones during both good and challenging times helps foster a sense of security and belonging. For instance offering words of affirmation helping a friend in need or celebrating someone's

achievements can strengthen the bonds of friendship.

5. Quality Time and Presence: Spending quality time together is vital for developing and nurturing relationships. It involves being fully present and engaged during interactions rather than being distracted or preoccupied. This could mean setting aside dedicated time to connect with loved ones engaging in meaningful conversations or partaking in enjoyable activities together. For example having regular family dinners organizing game nights with friends or going on walks with a partner can help create lasting memories and deepen relationships.

Section 2: Effective Communication Skills

Effective communication is essential for maintaining healthy relationships. It involves the exchange of information ideas and emotions in a clear and concise manner. In this section we will explore some key communication skills that can help enhance and nurture our relationships.

1. Active Listening: Active listening is an essential skill for effective communication. It involves fully concentrating on the speaker understanding their message and providing appropriate responses. Active listening requires giving our undivided attention maintaining eye contact and refraining from interrupting or making assumptions. By actively listening we show respect validate the speaker's perspective and create a supportive environment for open dialogue.

2. Clear and Concise Expression: Expressing ourselves clearly and concisely is crucial for effective communication. It involves

organizing our thoughts using appropriate language and delivering our message in a concise manner. Being clear and concise helps minimize misunderstandings and ensures that our message is accurately received. It is important to practice active self-reflection and choose words that are respectful kind and considerate of others' feelings.

3. Nonverbal Communication: Nonverbal communication plays a significant role in conveying messages and understanding emotions. It includes body language facial expressions tone of voice and gestures. Paying attention to nonverbal cues helps us better understand others' feelings and intentions. Similarly being aware of our own nonverbal communication can help us effectively express ourselves and avoid any unintended misinterpretations.

4. Empathetic Communication: Empathetic communication involves understanding and responding to the emotions and experiences of others. It requires us to put ourselves in the other person's shoes and respond with sensitivity and understanding. By acknowledging and validating their emotions we create a safe and supportive space for open communication. Empathetic communication builds trust strengthens relationships and fosters a sense of connection.

5. Conflict Resolution: Conflict is an inevitable part of any relationship. It is essential to develop effective conflict resolution skills to resolve differences and maintain healthy relationships. Approaching conflicts with an open mind active listening and empathy can help identify common ground and find mutually agreeable solutions. Additionally using "I" statements to

express our feelings and needs rather than placing blame can contribute to productive communication and resolution.

6. Mindful Communication: Mindful communication involves being present and fully attentive during interactions. It requires us to be aware of our thoughts emotions and reactions while engaging with others. Mindful communication helps us avoid unnecessary conflicts misunderstandings and hurtful remarks. By being mindful we can cultivate greater self-awareness and respond to others in a more thoughtful and compassionate manner.

In Conclusion:

Building strong connections and nurturing relationships is a continuous process that requires effort understanding and effective communication. Trust authenticity shared values empathy mutual respect quality time active listening clear expression nonverbal communication empathetic communication conflict resolution and mindful communication all play vital roles in fostering meaningful relationships. By incorporating these skills and concepts into our daily interactions we can create stronger bonds enhance our personal and professional lives and experience greater satisfaction and fulfillment.

Chapter 4: Pursuing Personal Growth

Section 1: Setting Meaningful Goals

Setting goals is an essential component of personal growth. Goals give us direction motivation and a sense of purpose. However not all goals are created equal. To truly pursue personal growth it is vital to set meaningful goals that align with our values aspirations and vision for the future. In this section we will explore the key principles of setting meaningful goals and provide examples to illustrate their application.

1. Reflect on Your Values and Aspirations:
Meaningful goals are rooted in personal values and aspirations. Take the time to reflect on what truly matters to you and what you want to achieve in different areas of your life. This reflection might involve contemplating your passions interests and long-term vision. For instance if you value creativity and have a passion for writing a meaningful goal might be to complete and publish a novel.

Example: Sarah is a marketing executive who feels unfulfilled in her current job. After some soul-searching she realizes that her true passion lies in helping others. She decides to set a meaningful goal of starting her own nonprofit organization to address the issue of homelessness in her community.

2. Set Specific and Measurable Goals:

Meaningful goals are clear specific and measurable. Vague goals like "be happier" or "get healthier" lack the necessary precision to track progress and stay motivated. Break down your broader aspirations into smaller concrete objectives that are easy to measure and evaluate. This approach allows you to track your progress adjust your strategies if needed and experience a sense of accomplishment along the way.

Example: Alex wants to improve his physical fitness. Instead of setting a general goal of "getting fit he sets a specific and measurable goal of running a 10k race within six months. This goal enables him to track his training progress monitor his running times and stay motivated throughout his fitness journey.

3. Make Goals Challenging but Realistic:

Meaningful goals strike a balance between being challenging and realistic. Setting overly ambitious goals that are beyond your current capabilities can lead to frustration and discouragement. On the other hand setting goals that are too easy may not sufficiently stretch your abilities hindering growth.

Example: Emily is an intermediate guitarist who wants to become proficient in playing jazz. Instead of aiming to become a world-renowned jazz guitarist within a year which would be unrealistic she sets a challenging but attainable goal of performing at a local jazz club within six months. This goal pushes her to develop her skills while taking into account her current level of expertise.

4. Ensure Goals are Relevant and Time-bound:
Meaningful goals are relevant to your overall vision and have a clear timeframe. Align your goals with your long-term aspirations and ensure they contribute to your personal growth. Additionally set deadlines for achieving your goals to maintain focus and prevent procrastination. Time-bound goals provide a sense of urgency and help prioritize your actions.

Example: John wants to transition from working in the corporate sector to becoming a freelance graphic designer. He sets relevant and time-bound goals of building a portfolio within three months networking with industry professionals within six months and securing his first freelance client within a year. These goals keep him motivated and on track towards his desired career transition.

5. Embrace both Process and Outcome Goals:
Meaningful goals encompass both process and outcome goals. Process goals focus on the steps actions and habits necessary to achieve the desired outcome. Outcome goals on the other hand represent the end result you want to attain. Balancing both types of goals ensures that you are not solely fixated on the end result but also enjoy the journey and growth that occurs along the way.

Example: Lisa is an aspiring artist who wants to enhance her painting skills. She sets a process goal of dedicating an hour each day towards practicing different techniques and experimenting with various mediums. Additionally she sets an outcome goal of entering a local art competition and gaining recognition for her work. By focusing on both the process and outcome Lisa ensures that she enjoys the daily practice while keeping her eye on the desired achievement.

Section 2: Cultivating a Growth Mindset

In the pursuit of personal growth developing a growth mindset is crucial. A growth mindset is a belief that skills abilities and intelligence can be developed through dedication effort and a willingness to learn. By cultivating a growth mindset we open ourselves up to continuous improvement embrace challenges and view failures as opportunities for growth. In this section we will delve into the principles of cultivating a growth mindset and provide examples to illustrate their application.

1. Embrace Challenges and Persistence:

A growth mindset perceives challenges as opportunities for growth rather than insurmountable obstacles. Embracing challenges allows us to stretch our abilities learn new skills and overcome setbacks. Cultivate persistence by adopting a problem-solving approach and viewing failures as stepping stones toward achieving mastery.

Example: Peter a software developer encounters a complex programming problem while working on a project. Instead of getting overwhelmed he views it as an opportunity to expand his skills and knowledge. He researches consults peers and persistently works to find a solution. Through this process he not only solves the specific problem but also enhances his programming abilities.

2. Cultivate a Love for Learning and Improvement:

A growth mindset values continuous learning and improvement. It recognizes that intelligence and abilities are not fixed but can be developed through effort and dedication. Embrace a love for learning by seeking opportunities to acquire new knowledge skills and perspectives. Engage in self-education attend seminars or workshops and explore new interests to expand your horizons.

Example: Sarah an accountant has a growth mindset and constantly pursues learning opportunities. She enrolls in a finance course to enhance her analytical skills and attends industry conferences to stay updated with the latest trends. Through this commitment to ongoing learning she not only improves her professional capabilities but also broadens her understanding of the field.

3. Value Effort and Resilience:

A growth mindset emphasizes the importance of effort and resilience in achieving success. It recognizes that mastery requires continuous practice perseverance and the willingness to bounce back from failures. Value the process of hard work and embrace challenges as a chance to improve rather than a measure of your worth.

Example: James a salesperson faces a series of rejections in his efforts to secure new clients. Instead of becoming discouraged he uses each rejection as an opportunity to improve his sales strategies. He seeks feedback refines his approach and persists in his efforts. Over time his resilience pays off as he learns valuable lessons from each setback and eventually secures new clients.

4. Foster a Positive Mindset and Self-belief:

A growth mindset nurtures a positive and optimistic outlook. It recognizes that setbacks and failures are temporary and can be overcome. Cultivate self-belief by focusing on your strengths accepting constructive criticism and maintaining a positive attitude even during challenging times. Develop resilience in the face of adversity and believe in your ability to grow and improve.

Example: Emma an aspiring entrepreneur faces numerous obstacles in launching her online business. Instead of dwelling on the challenges she maintains a positive mindset and believes in her ability to find solutions. She seeks advice from mentors conducts market research and adapts her business strategy when necessary. By staying optimistic and persistent she eventually builds a successful online venture.

5. Surround Yourself with Growth-oriented Individuals:

A growth mindset is reinforced by surrounding yourself with individuals who share similar values and encourage personal growth. Seek out relationships and communities that foster a growth-oriented mindset. Interact with people who inspire and challenge you facilitate your learning and provide support during your personal growth journey.

Example: Mark joins a mastermind group composed of individuals from different professional backgrounds who are all committed to personal growth. Through this group he engages in regular discussions shares insights and receives constructive feedback on his goals and progress. The supportive environment of the mastermind group fuels his motivation and provides valuable insights for his personal growth endeavors.

In conclusion pursuing personal growth involves setting meaningful goals and cultivating a growth mindset. Setting meaningful goals requires reflection on values and aspirations creating specific and measurable objectives making goals challenging yet attainable ensuring relevance and time-boundness and embracing both process and outcome goals. Cultivating a growth mindset involves embracing challenges valuing learning and improvement emphasizing effort and resilience fostering a positive mindset and self-belief and surrounding oneself with growth-oriented individuals. By incorporating these principles into our lives we can embark on an empowering journey of personal growth and development.

Chapter 5: Taking Care of Your Well-being

Section 1: Physical Health and Fitness

In today's fast-paced world it is crucial to prioritize our physical health and fitness. Taking care of our bodies not only improves overall well-being but also enhances our ability to handle daily challenges. This section delves into the importance of physical health and fitness and provides practical tips to maintain and improve them.

Physical health refers to the well-being of our bodies and encompasses various aspects such as nutrition exercise and regular check-ups. As the saying goes "You are what you eat nutrition plays a vital role in our physical well-being. A balanced diet that includes a variety of fruits vegetables whole grains lean proteins and healthy fats is essential for optimal health. It provides the necessary nutrients for growth development and functioning of the body.

For instance proteins are essential for building and repairing tissues carbohydrates provide energy for daily activities and vitamins and minerals support various bodily functions. Consuming a diverse range of nutrient-rich foods ensures we get a wide array of these essential nutrients. A well-rounded diet helps prevent deficiencies and reduces the risk of developing chronic diseases such as heart disease diabetes and certain cancers.

Moreover hydration is crucial for maintaining physical health. Our bodies are made up of around 60% water and staying adequately hydrated is essential for proper bodily functions. Water aids in digestion nutrient absorption temperature regulation and the elimination of waste products. It also supports healthy skin joints and organs. It is recommended to drink at least eight glasses of water per day or more if you engage in physical activity or live in a hot climate.

Exercise and physical activity are also integral to maintaining physical well-being. Regular exercise provides numerous benefits including improved cardiovascular health increased muscular strength and endurance enhanced flexibility and better mental health. Engaging in physical activity stimulates the release of endorphins which are natural mood boosters leading to reduced stress anxiety and depression.

There are various forms of exercise to choose from depending on your preferences and abilities. Aerobic exercises such as running swimming and cycling increase heart rate and promote cardiovascular fitness. Strength training exercises such as weightlifting or resistance training build muscle strength and improve bone density. Flexibility exercises like yoga or stretching enhance joint mobility and prevent muscle imbalances.

Finding an exercise routine that suits your lifestyle and interests is key to staying consistent. Aim for at least 150 minutes of moderate-intensity aerobic activity or 75 minutes of vigorous-intensity aerobic activity per week along with two or more days of strength training exercises. However it is essential to consult with a healthcare professional before starting any new exercise program especially if you have pre-existing medical conditions.

Additionally taking care of your physical health also involves regular check-ups and screenings with healthcare professionals. Prevention is crucial in maintaining good health and regular check-ups help identify potential health concerns before they become major problems. These check-ups may include routine physical examinations blood tests cholesterol screenings blood pressure measurements and cancer screenings depending on your age gender and medical history.

In summary taking care of your physical health involves maintaining a balanced diet staying hydrated engaging in regular exercise and monitoring your health through regular check-ups. By prioritizing these aspects you can enhance your overall well-being reduce the risk of chronic diseases and improve your quality of life.

Section 2: Mental and Emotional Wellness

In addition to physical health mental and emotional wellness is equally important for leading a fulfilling life. Our mental and emotional well-being affects how we think feel and behave influencing our relationships productivity and overall life satisfaction. This section explores the significance of mental and emotional wellness and provides strategies to nurture and maintain them.

Mental wellness refers to our cognitive and intellectual well-being. It encompasses aspects such as problem-solving skills coping mechanisms self-awareness and resilience. Building mental wellness requires actively engaging in activities that promote cognitive development and emotional intelligence.

One way to enhance mental wellness is through continuous learning. Learning new skills engaging in hobbies reading books or pursuing higher education fosters cognitive development expands knowledge and stimulates the brain. It enhances problem-solving abilities critical thinking skills and boosts self-confidence.

Additionally developing self-awareness is crucial for mental well-being. Self-awareness involves having a deep understanding of one's thoughts emotions and behaviors. It allows individuals to recognize their strengths and weaknesses set appropriate goals and make conscious choices aligned with their values and desires. Practices such as journaling mindfulness meditation and therapy can aid in cultivating self-awareness.

Furthermore building emotional intelligence is essential for managing emotions effectively. Emotional intelligence encompasses the ability to recognize and understand our own emotions as well as empathize with others. It involves skills such as emotional self-regulation empathy and effective communication. Developing emotional intelligence enables individuals to navigate social relationships resolve conflicts and maintain emotional equilibrium in challenging situations.

In addition to mental wellness emotional wellness focuses on our emotional state and how well we manage and express our emotions. Emotional wellness involves being aware of and expressing emotions appropriately as well as having healthy coping mechanisms for dealing with stress adversity and life challenges.

There are several strategies that can help nurture emotional wellness. Firstly it is important to develop healthy coping mechanisms for managing stress. Engaging in activities like meditation deep breathing exercises practicing gratitude and engaging in creative outlets (e.g art writing or music) can provide a sense of relaxation and release tension.

Secondly fostering healthy relationships and social connections is vital for emotional wellness. Having a strong support system of family and friends provides emotional validation encouragement and a sense of belonging. Regularly spending quality time with loved ones and engaging in activities that foster connection can significantly impact emotional well-being.

Thirdly finding ways to manage and express emotions effectively is crucial. This can involve seeking professional help such as therapy or counseling to gain insights and tools for emotional regulation. Additionally practicing mindfulness and self-compassion can help individuals acknowledge and validate their emotions without judgment.

Lastly maintaining a work-life balance is crucial for emotional well-being. High levels of stress from work-related pressures and excessive demands can negatively impact mental and emotional health. Setting boundaries prioritizing self-care and making time for leisure activities can help alleviate work-related stress and promote overall well-being.

In conclusion taking care of your mental and emotional wellness involves actively engaging in activities that promote cognitive development self-awareness and emotional intelligence. It also includes developing healthy coping mechanisms for managing stress fostering supportive relationships and maintaining a healthy work-life balance. By prioritizing mental and emotional well-being individuals can cultivate resilience emotional regulation and overall life satisfaction.

Chapter

Chapter 6: Finding Joy in Everyday Life

Section 1: Practicing Gratitude

Gratitude is a powerful practice that can transform our lives and help us find joy in everyday moments. When we are grateful we shift our focus from what we lack to what we have and this shift in perspective can have a profound impact on our overall well-being.

Practicing gratitude is simple a kind gesture from a friend or a delicious meal. By writing them down you reinforce the positive experiences in your mind.

2. Express gratitude to others: Take the time to express your gratitude to the people in your life presence and the positive impact they have on your life can deepen your relationships and create a more positive environment.

3. Practice mindfulness during daily activities: Engage your senses and fully immerse yourself in the present moment. For example when you're eating a meal savor each bite appreciate the colors and textures of your food and express gratitude for the nourishment it provides. By cultivating mindfulness you

can find joy in even the simplest activities.

4. Reflect on daily blessings: Before going to bed take a moment to reflect on the blessings you've experienced throughout the day. This act of gratitude can help you end your day on a positive note and set the tone for the following day.

5. Make a gratitude jar: Find a jar and some small slips of paper. Each day write down something you are grateful for and put it in the jar. Over time the jar will become a visual reminder of all the things you have to be grateful for and you can revisit it whenever you need a boost of joy and positivity.

Examples:

- Sarah starts her day by writing in her gratitude journal. She writes about the warm cup of coffee she enjoyed the sound of birds chirping outside her window and a heartfelt conversation she had with a close friend the previous day. By consciously acknowledging these moments of joy Sarah starts her day on a positive note.

- James decides to express his gratitude to his colleagues by writing a personalized thank-you note to each of them. He acknowledges their hard work support and camaraderie letting them know how much he appreciates them. This small act of gratitude strengthens the bond among the team members and fosters a positive work environment.

- Emma practices mindfulness while taking a walk in nature. She pays attention to the sights sounds and smells around her fully immersing herself in the present moment. She expresses gratitude for the beauty of the trees the peacefulness of the park and the fresh air she breathes. By being fully present Emma finds joy and appreciation in the simple act of being outside.

- Before going to bed Mark reflects on his daily blessings. He remembers the laughter shared with his family during dinner the encouraging words he received from a mentor and the feeling of accomplishment after completing a challenging task at work. By intentionally focusing on these positive experiences Mark ends his day feeling grateful and content.

- Sarah and her family create a gratitude jar. Each day they write down something they're grateful for and put it in the jar. Over time they accumulate a collection of slips of paper each representing a moment of gratitude. When they feel down or overwhelmed they take out some slips and read them aloud reminding themselves of the abundance of blessings in their lives.

Section 2: Embracing Mindfulness

Mindfulness is the practice of bringing our attention to the present moment with an attitude of curiosity non-judgment and acceptance. By shifting our focus from the past or future to the here and now we can find joy and contentment in the present moment meals. Notice the flavors textures and smells of your food. By fully engaging your senses you create a more mindful and enjoyable eating of her body. As she scans her body she becomes aware of areas of tension and consciously releases them bringing a sense of relaxation and grounding. This practice helps Sarah connect with her body and find joy in the physical sensations of being present.

-. By savoring his meal James taps into the joy of nourishment and cultivates a deeper sense of gratitude for the food he consumes.

- Emma decides to incorporate mindful walking into her daily routine. As she walks to work she pays attention to the physical sensations of each step the rhythm of her breath and the sights and sounds around her. By immersing herself in the present moment Emma finds joy in the simple act of walking and appreciates the beauty of her surroundings.

- Mark recognizes the need for a digital detox in his life. He sets aside dedicated time each day to disconnect from a deeper sense of appreciation and reconnect with the present moment. Whether it's expressing gratitude for a small act of kindness or savoring the sensations of a mindful walk these practices invite us to live fully and find joy in the everyday.

www.ingramcontent.com/pod-product-compliance
Lightning Source LLC
Chambersburg PA
CBHW062204160726
48282CB00027B/994
9788119786251